the weight of being right

by

No part of this publication may be reproduced, stored in a
retrieval system, or transmitted in any form or by any means
— electronic, mechanical, photocopying, recording, or
otherwise — without the prior written permission of the
publisher.

Published by Untold Imprint
www.sdarling-art.com

ISBN: 978-1-7641672-3-9
Printed in Australia.

This work examines psychological and behavioural patterns
related to certainty, conflict, responsibility, and
consequence.
It is observational in nature and grounded in established
principles of human behaviour, cognition, and social
interaction.

Any resemblance to real persons, living or dead, or to actual
events, is coincidental.

Being right is rarely examined beyond correctness.
Its psychological weight is discussed far less.

This book does not argue positions or assign fault.
It observes what occurs when truth meets human tolerance.

What follows is not meant to resolve tension,
but to make its structure visible.

Being right is often imagined as a resolution.
In practice, it rarely functions that way.

Correctness addresses accuracy, not outcome.
It clarifies what is true, but it does not determine how that
truth is received, absorbed, or tolerated.

Human beings do not experience information neutrally.
Information is filtered through identity, emotion, threat
perception, and social positioning.
As a result, being right more often introduces tension than
relief.

Evidence does not calm disagreement when disagreement
is not about evidence.
It escalates it.

When a belief is challenged, the nervous system responds
before cognition.
Contradiction is registered as threat long before it is
evaluated as data.
What follows is not analysis, but defence.

This is why correctness feels heavy.
It carries resistance, escalation, and consequence even
when it is accurate.

Being right does not fail because it is wrong.
It fails because truth operates independently of human
tolerance.

Accuracy does not guarantee understanding.
Clarity does not ensure repair.
Correctness does not absolve responsibility for what
follows.

The weight of being right is not moral.
It is mechanical.

Being right does not fail randomly.
It fails predictably.

Human beings do not interact with truth in isolation.
Information is processed through biological systems
designed for survival, not accuracy.

Before a claim is evaluated for validity, it is evaluated for
threat.

This assessment is automatic.
It occurs before reasoning, before reflection, before
intention.

Contradiction is not first interpreted as data.
It is interpreted as risk to identity, status, belonging, or
internal coherence.

Once threat is registered, the mind does not seek
understanding.
It seeks protection.

Defence precedes analysis.
Justification follows.

From this position, information is no longer evaluated for
truth.
It is evaluated for alignment.

Evidence that confirms belief feels safe.
Evidence that challenges belief feels hostile.

This response is not deliberate.
It is reflexive.

Cognitive systems evolved to preserve internal consistency
under pressure.
Not to revise beliefs in real time.

As a result, being right often activates the very mechanisms that prevent it from being absorbed.

Accuracy introduces instability.
Stability is prioritized.

This is not because truth is unwelcome.
It is because uncertainty is costly.

Revising a belief requires reorganization.
Reorganization requires effort, risk, and loss of coherence.

Certainty reduces that cost.

Beliefs are rarely held as isolated positions.
They are integrated into memory, identity, and narrative.

To be wrong is not merely to be mistaken.
It is to disrupt continuity.

For this reason, certainty is often protected long after it stops being useful.

Stability is preserved even when clarity is sacrificed.

What survives pressure is not the most accurate position, but the one that demands the least internal change.

Being right, in this context, becomes weight.

Not because it is wrong,
but because it requires adjustment.

Adjustment is not neutral.

It alters self-perception, past interpretation, and future expectation.

Being right does not determine outcome.
It initiates process.

Once introduced, that process unfolds according to human
tolerance, not logic.

Correction increases cognitive load.
Resistance reduces it.

This imbalance explains why belief systems harden under
pressure.

They simplify when complexity feels threatening.

What feels obvious is often what has survived longest,
not what has been examined most carefully.

Being right begins to feel heavy
when accuracy creates friction without control.

Truth clarifies.
It does not coordinate.

Correctness can expose reality
without resolving what follows from it.

The burden is not carried in knowing.
It is carried in what knowing disrupts.

This is the first cost of being right.

It appears before conflict,
before argument,
before consequence.

It appears as resistance.

Emotion is often mistaken for evidence.

Intensity is confused with accuracy.
Certainty is confused with validity.
Feeling strongly is treated as proof of being correct.

But emotion does not verify claims.
It only amplifies them.

Human emotion evolved to prioritize response, not evaluation.
It signals urgency, not precision.
It answers how something feels, not whether it is true.

This distinction is frequently ignored.

When emotion becomes the primary reference point, disagreement stops being analytical and becomes interpretive.
Statements are judged by resonance rather than accuracy.
What feels right is accepted long before it is examined.

This is how confidence emerges without verification.

Emotion collapses complexity into immediacy.
The present feeling overrides context.
History is filtered through sensation.

As a result, conclusions formed emotionally often feel undeniable while remaining untested.

This does not make them false.
It makes them unsupported.

An argument grounded primarily in emotion does not gain strength from intensity.
It gains fragility.

The moment emotion is challenged, the argument
experiences threat.
Correction feels like dismissal.
Clarification feels like invalidation.

At that point, the disagreement is no longer about truth.
It is about preserving the legitimacy of the feeling itself.

This is why emotional certainty resists evidence.
Not because the evidence is wrong,
but because accepting it would require downgrading the
authority of the feeling.

When feeling becomes the standard of correctness,
accuracy becomes optional.

And when accuracy becomes optional,
outcomes become unstable.

When emotion is treated as evidence,
being right stops functioning as resolution.

Accuracy no longer calms disagreement.
It destabilizes it.

This is where being right becomes heavy,
not because truth is unclear,
but because it now carries resistance, escalation, and
consequence
simply for existing.

Being right changes meaning the moment another person is involved.

Accuracy may remain intact, but tolerance does not.

Human interaction is not organized around truth-seeking.
It is organized around regulation, emotional, relational, and social.

In this context, information is not exchanged to establish correctness.
It is exchanged to maintain equilibrium.

When equilibrium is threatened, communication stops serving understanding.
It begins serving defence.

This is why disagreement escalates even when evidence improves.
The interaction is no longer responding to content.
It is responding to disruption.

Most conflict is not structured to be resolved.
It is structured to be stabilized.

Stability, in human systems, is often achieved through validation rather than accuracy.

To feel understood frequently matters more than to be correct.
Not because truth is irrelevant,
but because belonging is prioritized.

When emotion seeks acknowledgment, correction is experienced as interruption.
Evidence competes with validation.

This competition is rarely conscious.
It is procedural.

Providing proof in these moments does not reduce tension.
It intensifies it.

The interaction shifts from mutual regulation to positional conflict.
One side is now correcting.
The other is now defending.

Being right, in this setting, introduces asymmetry.

Correction places one person in the role of evaluator and the other in the role of subject.

This imbalance is often felt as threat,
even when the information is accurate
and the intent is neutral.

As a result, correctness becomes associated with dominance rather than clarity.

This is not because the information is aggressive.
It is because the structure of the interaction has changed.

The conversation is no longer about what is true.
It is about who holds position.

Once this shift occurs, escalation becomes likely.

Listening gives way to preparation.
Responses are assembled before understanding is complete.

Information is filtered for advantage, not coherence.

This is why many arguments continue even after the facts are settled.
Resolution was never the organizing goal.

What persists is not disagreement,
but the need to restore balance.

Being right does not restore balance.
It disrupts it.

Correctness can settle a claim
while leaving the relationship unstable.

In these moments, being right feels costly
not because it is incorrect,
but because it fails to perform the function the interaction
requires.

Truth clarifies.
It does not regulate.

And regulation is what most human conflict is attempting to
achieve.

This is the second cost of being right.

It appears as distance.
As withdrawal.
As unresolved tension.

Not because the truth was wrong,
but because it arrived without coordination.

Being right does not only challenge emotion.
It challenges arrangement.

Truth is tolerated most easily when it is harmless.
When it confirms what already exists.
When it does not require redistribution.

Resistance to being right is often explained as discomfort.
But discomfort alone does not account for the intensity of
the response.

What is threatened is not just feeling.
It is position.

Clarity destabilizes systems that depend on ambiguity.
It removes flexibility from roles that were never meant to be
examined.
It exposes benefits that required silence to persist.

This is why truth is welcomed selectively.

It is praised in theory,
but resisted in practice
the moment it alters who carries responsibility
and who absorbs cost.

Being right becomes intolerable when it forces
renegotiation.

When it asks who benefits.
Who is protected.
Who has been spared consequence by vagueness.

In many environments, ambiguity is not an accident.
It is functional.

It allows problems to persist without ownership.
It allows authority without accountability.
It allows outcomes without attribution.

Being right interrupts this.

It removes plausible deniability.
It collapses shared confusion into individual responsibility.

This is when being right becomes socially expensive.

Not because it is disruptive,
but because it is corrective.

Correction threatens leverage.

It exposes arrangements that only worked
because they were never named.

This is why timing is invoked.
Why tone is questioned.
Why intent is scrutinized more than accuracy.

These are not responses to truth.
They are strategies to delay its consequences.

Being right does not simply clarify what is true.
It clarifies what must now change.

And change redistributes cost.

When the cost becomes visible, resistance intensifies.

Not everyone opposes truth because they doubt it.
Some oppose it because they understand it perfectly.

They know exactly what it will require.

This is the weight most people underestimate.

Being right does not just carry emotional burden.
It carries structural consequence.

It threatens comfort that was never neutral.
It destabilizes benefit that was never acknowledged.

And once that destabilization begins,
being right is no longer a matter of accuracy.

It becomes a matter of endurance.

Being right does not end responsibility.
It often initiates it.

Correctness may resolve uncertainty,
but it does not resolve consequence.

Once truth is established, the question shifts.
Not *is this accurate?*
But *what does this accuracy now require?*

Most people experience this shift as unfair.

They expect correctness to function as closure.
Instead, it produces obligation.

Truth removes ambiguity.
And with ambiguity gone, choice becomes visible.

What follows is not relief,
but exposure.

Responsibility becomes unavoidable once alternatives
disappear.
When the facts are clear, so are the options that were
ignored.

This is where resistance intensifies.

People do not avoid responsibility because they are
ignorant.
They avoid it because responsibility demands response, not
explanation.

Explanation preserves position.
Responsibility requires movement.

Being right often delays this movement.

It provides a place to stand
when what is actually required is change.

Justification thrives where responsibility would otherwise
begin.
It converts consequence into narrative.

The story becomes more important than the repair.

This is why accountability feels heavy.
It is not punitive.
It is directional.

It points forward when many would rather remain oriented
toward the past.

Responsibility does not ask how something happened.
It asks what happens next.

Intent becomes irrelevant once impact is present.
Accuracy does not dissolve outcome.

Being right does not neutralize damage.
It clarifies it.

This clarification is often experienced as loss.

Loss of moral leverage.
Loss of defensibility.
Loss of shared blame.

Responsibility isolates.

It cannot be distributed without distortion.
It cannot be postponed without cost.

When people resist accountability, they often describe the
resistance as exhaustion.

As unfairness.
As imbalance.

But what they are reacting to is gravity.

Responsibility is weight that cannot be argued away.
It accumulates quietly until it is carried or transferred.

Being right increases this weight
because it removes uncertainty as shelter.

Once clarity exists, inaction becomes decision.

Avoidance becomes choice.
Delay becomes participation.

This is why correctness often feels heavier than ignorance.

Ignorance allows drift.
Being right demands orientation.

And orientation requires alignment between knowledge and
behaviour.

That alignment is rare.

Not because people do not value truth,
but because truth destabilizes arrangements that once
functioned.

Being right exposes the cost of maintaining what no longer
fits.

That cost is often paid reluctantly,
or not at all.

When it is not paid, it does not disappear.
It relocates.

The burden shifts outward.
Onto relationships.
Onto environments.
Onto others.

This is the third cost of being right.

Not conflict.
Not distance.

But consequence deferred and redistributed.

Consequence does not wait for agreement.

It unfolds regardless of how truth is received,
or whether responsibility is acknowledged.

This is the part rarely discussed.

Being right is often imagined as power.
In practice, it functions more like exposure.

Once something is known,
it cannot be unknown.

Once a pattern is seen,
it cannot be unseen.

This is where being right becomes irreversible.

Not because action must immediately follow,
but because denial now requires effort.

Maintenance replaces ignorance.

The energy once spent not knowing
is now spent avoiding response.

This effort accumulates.

Avoidance is not neutral.
It consumes attention, distorts priorities, and narrows
choice.

The longer responsibility is delayed,
the more complex the consequences become.

Not because the situation worsens on its own,
but because time introduces additional variables.

More people become involved.
More systems adapt around the avoidance.
More damage is normalized.

Being right early is rarely rewarded.
It is often resented.

It disrupts arrangements before alternatives are prepared.

As a result, correctness is frequently treated as impatience.
As insensitivity.
As a failure to be considerate of timing.

But timing is rarely the real objection.

What is resisted is not the truth,
but the obligation it introduces.

Irreversibility removes negotiation.

Once consequence is visible,
the question is no longer *whether* something must change.

It is *who* will absorb the cost.

This is where being right becomes isolating.

Alignment with truth separates those willing to adapt
from those invested in preservation.

Neutrality collapses.

Silence becomes position.
Delay becomes endorsement.

At this stage, being right no longer feels like accuracy.
It feels like separation.

People begin to distance themselves
not from the truth itself,
but from the weight attached to it.

This is why being right is often lonely.

Not because others disagree,
but because agreement would require participation.

Participation would require sacrifice.

Sacrifice exposes priorities.

And priorities, once exposed,
cannot be reconciled without loss.

This is the final cost of being right.

Not argument.
Not conflict.
Not responsibility.

But the recognition that some truths, once carried,
cannot be set down without leaving something behind.

Being right is often mistaken for the objective.

In reality, it is usually a by-product,
not an outcome.

In conflict, especially relational conflict,
being right rarely produces resolution.

It produces escalation.

This is because conflict is not governed by accuracy.
It is governed by perception, threat, and regulation.

Confirmation bias ensures that people do not enter
disagreement to be corrected.
They enter it to preserve coherence.

Once a position is taken, information is no longer evaluated
neutrally.
It is filtered for compatibility.

Evidence that supports one's view feels clarifying.
Evidence that challenges it feels hostile.

This response is not intellectual.
It is biological.

Contradiction activates threat detection before reasoning
engages.
The nervous system responds to opposition as instability,
not as information.

This is why facts rarely soften conflict.
They harden it.

Providing evidence during emotional disagreement does
not resolve uncertainty.
It confirms opposition.

The moment proof is introduced,
the interaction shifts from connection to contest.

One person becomes correct.
The other becomes cornered.

In relational conflict, particularly between men and women
this shift is decisive.

When emotion is seeking validation,
accuracy is experienced as dismissal.

The more evidence is provided,
the more the emotional signal is overridden.

Being right, in this context, does not feel clarifying.
It feels silencing.

This is why escalation follows.

Not because the facts are wrong,
but because the interaction is no longer about facts.

It is about safety, recognition, and position.

Confirmation bias ensures that once escalation begins,
new information is recruited only to defend the existing
stance.

The argument becomes self-sealing.

Each side feels more justified
precisely because they are no longer listening.

At this point, being right has already failed.

Not morally.
Mechanically.

The goal was never correctness.
The goal was regulation.

Connection does not collapse because truth was
introduced.
It collapses because truth was treated as the endpoint.

Being right is not resolution.
It is not repair.
It is not understanding.

It is simply accuracy.

When accuracy is pursued as victory,
it guarantees distance.

The conflict ends not because clarity was reached,
but because tolerance was exceeded.

This is the mistake.

Being right is never the end of the line.
It is the point where responsibility begins.

And in relationships,
responsibility is not carried by facts.

It is carried by how truth is held,
timed,
and delivered.

Knowing does not automatically lead to action.

In many cases, it leads to hesitation.

Once the weight of being right is understood, behaviour
changes, not toward alignment, but toward avoidance.

Not because the truth disappeared,
but because living in accordance with it proved heavier than
anticipated.

At this stage, the question is no longer *what is true*.

It becomes *what is tolerable*.

People rarely abandon truth outright.
They postpone it.

They delay action while calling it consideration.
They soften language while calling it diplomacy.
They reduce urgency while calling it patience.

These behaviours appear reasonable on the surface.
They are often praised.

But they serve a specific function.

They allow the individual to remain correct without
becoming accountable.

Silence becomes a strategy.

Not because there is nothing to say,
but because saying it would force movement.

Delay becomes justification.

Time is used to diffuse responsibility rather than to clarify it.

Complexity is emphasized not to understand the situation better,
but to avoid committing to a direction.

At this point, correctness becomes compartmentalized.

It is acknowledged internally
and neutralized externally.

Truth is held privately while behaviour remains unchanged.

This creates a split.

One part of the person knows what is accurate.
Another part continues to operate as if that knowledge does not yet apply.

This split is not accidental.

It is the price paid to avoid consequence.

People tell themselves they are waiting for the right moment.
But the right moment is often defined as the moment when consequence no longer exists.

That moment rarely arrives.

The longer alignment is delayed, the heavier the truth becomes.

Not because it grows more complex,
but because the cost of acting on it compounds.

Each delay adds another layer of implication.
Each silence becomes a decision retroactively.

This is how people become trapped by what they already know.

They are no longer choosing between right and wrong.
They are choosing between disruption now or damage later.

Most choose later.

Not because it is better,
but because it feels less visible.

This is the quiet cost of being right.

Truth does not disappear when it is ignored.
It accumulates.

It presses inward.

It alters posture, tone, patience, and tolerance.

People become guarded without understanding why.
Resentment grows without clear attribution.
Fatigue appears without obvious cause.

The weight is not emotional.

It is behavioural.

Energy is spent maintaining misalignment.

Justifying inaction.
Explaining delay.
Defending neutrality.

This is why being right often feels isolating.

Not because others rejected the truth,
but because alignment would require stepping away from
familiar roles.

From relationships that depend on silence.
From systems that reward compliance.
From dynamics that benefit from ambiguity.

At this point, being right no longer feels like insight.

It feels like an obligation with no obvious reward.

This is where many people stop.

Not because they changed their mind,
but because they calculated the cost.

They remain correct,
but no longer coherent.

They carry the truth privately
and perform contradiction publicly.

This is not hypocrisy.

It is adaptation.

A way of surviving environments that cannot absorb clarity
without restructuring.

But survival comes with consequence.

The longer this split persists, the harder alignment
becomes.

Eventually, action feels impossible
not because it is wrong,
but because too much time has passed without it.

The truth is still accurate.
The opportunity to act cleanly is gone.

This is the final behavioural cost of being right.

Not punishment.
Not backlash.

But inertia reinforced by delay.

And at that point, the weight is no longer abstract.

It is lived.

Truth is not always rejected because it is unclear.

Often, it is rejected because it is inconvenient.

There is a point where confusion ends and preference
begins.
Where the facts are sufficiently understood,
the implications are sufficiently visible,
and the resistance continues anyway.

At that point, disbelief is no longer an error.

It is a decision.

People rarely say they are choosing a personal truth over a
factual one.
They say they are being nuanced.
They say the situation is complex.
They say there are other perspectives to consider.

These statements are not always false.
But they often function as cover.

Once truth requires change, tolerance for it narrows.

When accuracy threatens identity, comfort, or advantage,
a more survivable version is selected.

Not because it is more accurate,
but because it is more liveable.

This is how personal truth forms.

It is not fabricated from nothing.
It is edited.

Facts that demand adjustment are softened.
Details that imply responsibility are minimized.

Contradictions that require action are reframed as misunderstandings.

The resulting narrative feels coherent enough to inhabit, even if it no longer aligns fully with reality.

This process is rarely conscious.

People do not experience it as dishonesty.
They experience it as preservation.

Preservation of self-image.
Preservation of relationships.
Preservation of position.

But preservation is not neutral.

Choosing what feels tolerable over what is accurate does not suspend consequence.
It delays it.

Truth does not need belief to remain operative.
It continues to shape outcomes even when it is denied.

This is why personal truth often feels stable in the short term
and destabilizing in the long term.

It postpones discomfort,
but compounds cost.

Eventually, the difference between what is believed
and what is true
begins to express itself behaviourally.

Decisions feel harder to justify.
Explanations require more maintenance.
Energy is spent defending positions that no longer feel solid.

At this stage, people often describe feeling misunderstood.
But what they are experiencing is misalignment.

The internal narrative no longer matches the external
demands of reality.

This is the final cost of preference.

Not that truth was ignored,
but that it was known and set aside.

Once that choice is made, being right becomes heavier.

Because the weight is no longer carried by ignorance.
It is carried by avoidance.

Being right does not arrive as resolution.

There is no moment where clarity announces itself as success.
No signal that the burden has been carried correctly.
No reward for having seen what others avoided.

What arrives instead is quiet.

A narrowing of options.
A thinning of excuses.
The collapse of plausible deniability.

Being right simplifies the world in ways that feel destabilizing.

What once felt complex becomes fixed.
What once felt negotiable becomes immovable.
What once felt shared becomes yours alone.

This is not empowerment.
It is compression.

Possibility contracts.
Flexibility disappears.
Choice becomes exposed.

Once something is known, pretending otherwise requires effort.
Once consequence is understood, delay becomes participation.

This is why ambiguity is preferred.

Ambiguity allows movement without direction.
Engagement without ownership.
Involvement without cost.

Being right removes that shelter.

It replaces comfort with obligation.
It replaces explanation with responsibility.

And responsibility is not generous.

Correctness does not reward the person who carries it.
It assigns them weight.

Often, that weight is to act without consensus.
To move without validation.
To absorb consequence without recognition.

This is where the fantasy collapses.

Truth does not guarantee alignment.
Clarity does not produce unity.
Accuracy does not repair what it exposes.

Sometimes, being right only reveals what will not change.
Sometimes, it clarifies limits rather than solutions.

The weight of being right is not found in disagreement,
but in what must now be done with no illusion left to protect
you.

There is no relief here.
Only precision.

Precision about responsibility.
Precision about consequence.
Precision about cost.

And once that precision exists, neutrality disappears.

You either carry what you now know,
or you devote your energy to pretending you don't.

That is the final decision.

Not between right and wrong,
but between avoidance and ownership.

The weight of being right
is not the truth itself.

It is living in alignment with it
after every alternative has failed.

what are you still protecting by being right?

www.ingramcontent.com/pod-product-compliance
Lightning Source LLC
Chambersburg PA
CBHW060524280326
41933CB00014B/3100